Words to Love by...

MOTHER TERESA

To [illegible]

— [illegible] and [illegible] with you

— [illegible]

[illegible signature]

AVE MARIA PRESS   **Notre Dame, Indiana**

Acknowledgment

The interviews on which this book is based were conducted by Michael Nabicht and Gaynell Cronin, who spent several weeks with Mother Teresa in Calcutta while making the film WORK OF LOVE. The text of the book was compiled and edited by Frank J. Cunningham. Photography is by the Rev. Patrick Delahanty.

The film, WORK OF LOVE, is produced and distributed by Ikonographics, PO Box 4454, Louisville, Kentucky 40204.

A portion of the receipts from the sale of this book will be given to the Missionaries of Charity.

© 1983 by Ave Maria Press, Notre Dame, Indiana 46556.

International Standard Book Number: 087793-260-3 (Cloth)
087793-261-1 (Paper)
Library of Congress Catalog Card Number: 82-73373
Printed and bound in the United States of America.

Cover and text design: Elizabeth French
Cover photo: Rev. Patrick Delahanty

Contents

Introduction

Mother Teresa of Calcutta has a dream—that before they die all people will know that they are loved. She devotes her life to making this dream a reality.

She tells a story of walking past an open drain and catching a glimpse of something moving in it. She investigated and found a dying man whom she took back to a home where he could die in love and peace.

"I live like an animal in the streets," the man told her. "Now I will die like an angel."

"How wonderful to see a person die in love," she exclaims, "with the joy of love, the perfect peace of Christ on his face."

Mother Teresa began picking up the dying in the streets of Calcutta in 1952. Since then she and the members of her order of sisters, the Missionaries of Charity, have provided love and comfort for over 40,000 people abandoned in the streets. Paradoxically, as a result of the love and care of the sisters, over half the people recovered.

There are only a few details to her life story. She was born Agnes Boyaxhui in Skopje, Yugoslavia, in 1910. She joined the Loretto nuns in Ireland in 1928 and within a year was sent to India to do her novitiate and to begin teaching at St. Mary's High School in Calcutta.

She taught there for nearly 20 years, but in 1946 on the way to her annual retreat, she says, "I heard the call to give up all and to follow him into the slums and to serve among the poorest of the poor."

She sought and acquired release from the Loretto sisters and in 1948 left the convent to lead the life of a religious among the poor, and under obedience to the Archbishop of Calcutta. She began a school in the slums where she taught older children. She also learned some basic medicine from the American Medical Mission Sisters and went into the homes of the sick to treat them. It wasn't long before former students from St. Mary's and a few volunteers were working with her.

In 1952 she came across an abandoned woman, dying in the street and being consumed by rats and ants. She picked the woman up and took her to a hospital, but the hospital couldn't help. Mother Teresa then took her to city authorities and asked for help to provide a place for this woman and others left to die in the streets.

A health official took her to a building located next to a temple dedicated to the Hindu goddess Kali. Intended as a hostel for pilgrims visiting the temple, the building was not being used. He offered her the use of it and within a day she had people there, and had started the home for the destitute sick and dying—now known as Kalighat.

Over the years she expanded her work enormously to minister to almost every type of suffering she encountered —providing shelter and finding homes for orphans, feeding the hungry and clothing the naked, running family-planning clinics and mobile dispensaries, and caring for thousands of lepers.

She founded the Missionaries of Charity which now has more than 3000 members working in 52 countries—in such diverse places as Rome and Addis Ababa, the Bronx and Jenkins, Kentucky. The Missionaries take the usual religious vows of poverty, chastity and obedience. But they also take a fourth vow, one of "wholehearted, free service to the poorest of the poor." In an era of declining religious vocations, the Missionaries are thriving. The explanation is simple according to Mother Teresa. "There are women in this work who are still looking for a life of prayer, poverty and sacrifice."

Mother Teresa's work has earned her worldwide recognition. She is considered one of the world's most admired women and in 1979 she was awarded the Nobel Peace Prize.

Such notoriety has not affected her demeanor or the way she lives. She goes barefoot whenever possible and sleeps on the floor of an open dormitory with other sisters and novices. She eats lightly and uses only cold water from a pump. Like all Missionaries of Charity she owns only two white cotton saris and washes her own laundry and dishes.

Visitors are struck by her simplicity and frugality as they perhaps watch her comb the hair of a young Indian girl, or turn the lights out during the parts of the Mass at the convent when there is no reading. Such an action is far from a compulsion. Rather it is indicative of a way of life. "No money that is given to the poor," she explains, "should be wasted on our electricity. We use only what we absolutely need."

With her notoriety has come, however, a demanding worldwide travel and speaking schedule. She does not raise funds for her community through these activities, though invariably her hosts inform the audience that donations can be sent to the Helpers of the Missionaries of Charity. She speaks simply and eloquently, illustrating her message of love of Jesus and humankind with anecdotes from her personal experience. Her message is sprinkled with many now familiar phrases that always bear repeating: "We do it for Jesus, to Jesus and with Jesus," "something beautiful for God," "give until it hurts," "serve Jesus in the distressing disguise of the poor."

Inevitably, someone overwhelmed by her dedication, will ask, "What can I do to help?" Her response is always the same, a response that reveals the clarity of her vision. Respond individually, where we are. "Just begin, one, one, one," she urges. "Begin at home by saying something good to your child, to your husband or to your wife. Begin by helping someone in need in your community, at work, or at school. Begin by making whatever you do something beautiful for God." As a social critic she replaces indignation with service.

Little seems to affect or intimidate her during these long and tiring periods of public appearance. She seems to always project the joy that is such an important element of the lives of all Missionaries of Charity.

She lives the joy of the resurrection, and joy and cheerfulness is central to her work. "Do what you do with a happy heart," she admonishes. The dying man in the gutter is Jesus in distressing disguise. "Whenever you meet Jesus, smile at him," she tells her sisters. "If you don't want to smile at Jesus, then pack up and go home."

Even a crusty, jaded press corps leaves her unfazed. In a recent press conference in a midwestern American city she was asked questions revolving around changes in the church in recent years, femininism and women's roles, the spiritual condition of the Western world, economics and the use of media to spread the gospel.

She either flat-out says, "I don't know anything about that," or she brings the question around to her vision. "If you do this work for the praise of men you could only do it for a year and no more. Only if you do it for Jesus can you go on." She and her Missionaries of Charity live the gospel in its most literal and radical form.

For the members of the press corps, a least in this particular session, she was a very different experience. They are not used to hearing someone say that she loves Jesus and is motivated by him, or sustained by the Eucharist and prayer. A few are struck. You can see it in their eyes. Most miss the message completely and respond to her as a naive lady trying to effect impossible social change. They cannot grasp that this woman has a personal relationship with Jesus and has responded to what he asks. Like society as a whole, they admire and praise her and her work, but miss the simplicity of her motivation.

Some who know Mother Teresa, who have spent time with her, feel she is a gift to our times. Perhaps she is also one of those occasional historical figures who comes along to remind us of the message of the gospel, to remind us of what the Father expects.

Agnes Boyaxhui complains about words. "Too many words," she says. "Let them just see what we do." Yet she continues to speak, patiently repeating the essentials of her vision.

The few words that follow—her words—hopefully will offer insight and understanding of the woman and her work. They will certainly remind all who read them of the essentials of the gospel.

All souls need to be converted.
And if they accept God in their lives
   they are converted.
To grow in holiness is a sign of conversion.
To grow in likeness of Christ is a sign of conversion.

If they reject him,
if they reject his presence
then they are supposed to try and try again
until they find him.

One

Jesus —
the Bread
of Life

Where Jesus is . . . there is joy
                        there is peace
                        there is love.
And that is why he made himself the Bread of Life
    to be our life of love and joy.
No one else can give what he gives
    and he is there all the time.
We have only to realize that.

Jesus has said very clearly:
>   I am the love to be loved
>   I am the life to be lived
>   I am the joy to be shared
>   I am the bread to be eaten
>   I am the blood to be drunk
>   I am the truth to be told
>   I am the light to be lit
>   I am the peace to be given.

Jesus is everything.

Jesus is always there . . .
     to love
     to share
     to be the joy of our life.
Jesus' love for us is unconditional
                         tender
                         forgiving
                         complete.
Without counting the cost
without measuring
without anything
he gives until it hurts.

Love, to be true, has to hurt.
A little child who gives up sugar for
     three days, loves until it hurts.
It hurt God, the Father, to give his son.
It hurt Jesus to love you and me.

Just allow people to see Jesus in you
  to see how you pray
  to see how you lead a pure life
  to see how you deal with your family
  to see how much peace there is in your family.
Then you can look straight into their eyes and say,
   "This is the way."
You speak from life, you speak from experience.

A few weeks ago there was a French girl from Paris University here. She is working on her Ph.D.

Suddenly she comes and tells me, "I have found Jesus."

I said, "Where did you find Jesus?"

"In the home for the dying."

And I said, "What did you do when you found Jesus?"

"I went to confession and communion."

It had been 15 years since she last did this.

And I said, "What else did you do?"

"I sent a telegram to my parents to tell them I found Jesus."

All the way from Paris . . . then contact with these people (in the home) and she found Jesus.

Really, God is very much in love with us.

For example, we go to confession full of sin and come out without sin. How could there be greater love? This is something the human mind cannot understand.

That is why Jesus continually says, "Love as I have loved you." We must be able to forgive like that.

For our Lady, the annunciation was when Jesus came into her life—that was her first communion day. And she did something very beautiful.

As she realized Jesus was with her, she went in haste, immediately, to see her cousin Elizabeth who was with child. And we know what that unborn child did:

Leapt with joy at the presence of Christ.

He was the first to declare Jesus had come.

It's wonderful to think that it was an unborn child that had the first privilege to proclaim.

We *Do It for Jesus*

Two

The work we do is only our love for Jesus in action.
And that action is our wholehearted and free service
        —the gift to the poorest of the poor—
to Christ in the distressing disguise of the poor.

If we pray the work . . .
        if we do it to Jesus
        if we do it for Jesus
        if we do it with Jesus . . .
that's what makes us content.

That is why I feel the Missionaries of Charity are real
contemplatives in the heart of the world.

I do this because I believe I am doing it for Jesus.
I am very sure that this is his work.
I am very sure.
I am very sure that it is he and not me.

How do we prove that we love God?

How do we prove that we love Christ with undivided love and chastity?

By giving wholehearted free service to the poorest of the poor.

We believe it is to Jesus.

This thing, if it were not for Jesus, would not be worth doing.

The Minister of Social Welfare is a Hindu gentleman in New Delhi. One day we were talking and he said, "You and I are doing the same social work. But there is a great difference between you and us. We are doing it *for* something and you are doing it *to* somebody."

And I think that is all.

That explains the reason for our work.

If you are preoccupied with people who are talking about the poor, you scarcely have time to talk to the poor. Some people talk about hunger, but they don't come and say, "Mother, here is five rupees. Buy food for these people." But they can give a most beautiful lecture on hunger.

I had the most extraordinary experience once in Bombay. There was a big conference about hunger. I was supposed to go to that meeting and I lost the way. Suddenly I came to that place, and right in front of the door to where hundreds of people were talking about food and hunger, I found a dying man.

I took him out and I took him home.

He died there.

He died of hunger.

And the people inside were talking about how in 15 years we will have so much food, so much this, so much that, and that man died.

See the difference?

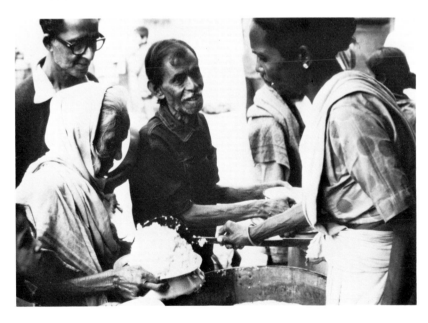

We are trying to make our communities another
Nazareth, where Jesus can come and rest awhile.

Jesus had to become poor to be able to be one of us.
    He had to become small
    he had to become weak
    he had to become helpless
    he had to become dependent
    he had to become lonely,
        to feel unwanted, unloved, uncared for.
Except for his mother, nobody knew who he was. He was
regarded as the son of Joseph the Carpenter, and people
said nothing good could come from Nazareth.

And I think this is what we are trying to do . . . to be
that small one, that helpless one so that we can be able to
proclaim that God loves the world. That is the Good News
we are trying to proclaim.

Our vocation is to belong to Jesus with the conviction that nothing and nobody can separate us from the love of Christ.

Jesus has offered his lifelong, faithful, personal friendship in tenderness and love to each one of us. He has espoused us to himself.

So now by our presence we put that love, that undivided love for Christ in chastity, into an action.

Our love in action is this service to the poorest of the poor.

Our presence is our prayer life
> our union with Christ
> our oneness with Christ
> our living the life of the Bread of Life
> in action.

Jesus went about doing good.

And we are trying to imitate him now because I believe that God loves the world through us.

Just as he sent Jesus to be his love, his presence in the world, so today he is sending us.

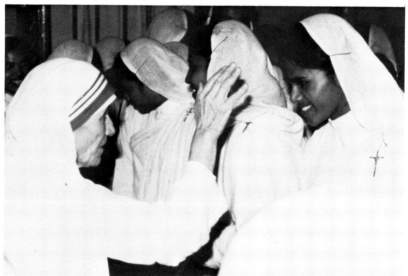

Sharing, thoughtfulness . . . help build community life.
Doing small things for the great love of each other
  maybe just a smile
  maybe just carrying a bucket of water
  maybe just thoughtfulness at the table.
These are small things . . . small things.

And that continual sharing with each other, continual
relating to each other . . .
  Mass together
  Eucharist together
  adoration together
  doing penance together
to be able to share the suffering and understand the suffering of our people. We really do everything together, and I think that being together is our strength.

The sisters are always smiling and happy.
We are so free . . . we are so free.

I think people are so preoccupied with material difficulties. In the industrial world where people are supposed
to have so much, I find that many people, while dressed
up, are really, really poor.

By having nothing we will be able to give everything
    —through the freedom of poverty.

The *Family of God*

Three

The same loving hand that has created you
    has created me.
If he is your Father
    he must be my Father also.
We all belong to the same family.
Hindus, Muslims and all peoples are our brothers and
    sisters.
They too are the children of God.

Our work among the Hindus proclaims that
    God loves them
    God has created them
    they are my brothers and sisters.
Naturally I would like to give them the joy of what I
       believe
    but that I cannot do;
    only God can.
Faith is a gift of God
    but God does not force himself.

Christians, Muslims, Hindus, believers and nonbelievers
    have the opportunity with us to do works of love
    have the opportunity with us to share the joy of
       loving and come to realize God's presence.
Hindus become better Hindus.
Catholics become better Catholics.
Muslims become better Muslims.

Prayer *Changes Our Hearts*

Four

Change your hearts . . .
Unless we change our hearts we are not converted.
Changing places is not the answer.
Changing occupations is not the answer.
The answer is to change our hearts.

And how do we change?
    By praying.

The most important thing to do to change my
    heart is confession. After confession,
    holy communion.
And then I am full of peace.

Prayer is joy
prayer is love
prayer is peace.
You cannot explain it
you must experience prayer.
It is not impossible.
God gives it for the asking.
"Ask and you shall receive."
The father knows what to give his children
—how much more our heavenly father knows.

The beginning of prayer is silence . . . God speaking in the silence of the heart. And then we start talking to God from the fullness of the heart. And he listens.

The beginning of prayer is scripture . . . we listen to God speaking. And then we begin to speak to him again from the fullness of our heart. And he listens.

That is really prayer. Both sides listening and both sides speaking.

To be able to pray we need a pure heart.
With a pure heart we can see God.
We need a pure heart to love Jesus
and to live his life—
　　　the life of Lazarus
　　　the life of Mary
　　　the life of the holy Eucharist
　　　the life of the passion
whatever he chooses for our life.

It is not we who live
it is he who has to live in us.
Allowing him to live his life in us
　　　is prayer.
And the more we allow him
　　　the more we grow in likeness of Christ.

We need prayer to understand God's love for us.
You have to read that beautiful passage in Isaiah where
God speaks and says:
>"I have called you by name. You are mine.
>Water will not drown you, fire will not burn you.
>I will give up nations for you. You are
>precious to me."

We are precious to him.
>That man dying in the street—precious to him
>that millionaire—precious to him
>that sinner—precious to him.

Because he loves us.

The fruit of prayer is a deepening of faith.
And the fruit of faith is love.
And the fruit of love is service.

But to be able to pray we need silence
        silence of the heart.
The soul needs time to go away and pray
        to use the mouth
        to use the eyes
        to use the whole body.
And if we don't have that silence
        then we don't know how to pray.

We have ups and downs and sickness and suffering.
That is part of the cross.
Anyone who imitates him to the full
     must share in his passion also.
That is why we need prayer
that is why we need the Bread of Life
that is why we have adoration
that is why we do penance.

We complicate prayer as we complicate many things.
It is to love Jesus with undivided love—for you, for
me, for all of us. And that undivided love is put into action
when we do as Jesus said, "Love as I have loved you."

I think if we can spread this prayer, if we can translate it into our lives, it will make all the difference. It is so full of Jesus. It has made a great difference in the lives of the Missionaries of Charity.

Dear Jesus,
Help us to spread your fragrance everywhere we go.
Flood our souls with your spirit and life.
Penetrate and possess our whole being so utterly
    that our lives may only be a radiance of yours.
Shine through us
and be so in us
that every soul we come in contact with
    may feel your presence in our soul.
Let them look up and see no longer us
but only Jesus.
Stay with us
and then we shall begin to shine as you shine,
so to shine as to be light to others.
The light, O Jesus, will be all from you.
None of it will be ours.
It will be you shining on others through us.
Let us thus praise you in the way you love best
    by shining on those around us.
Let us preach you without preaching
    not by words, but by our example
    by the catching force
    the sympathetic influence of what we do
    the evident fullness of the love our hearts bear to
        you
                                    Amen.

Five

The Family — a Place to Learn Jesus

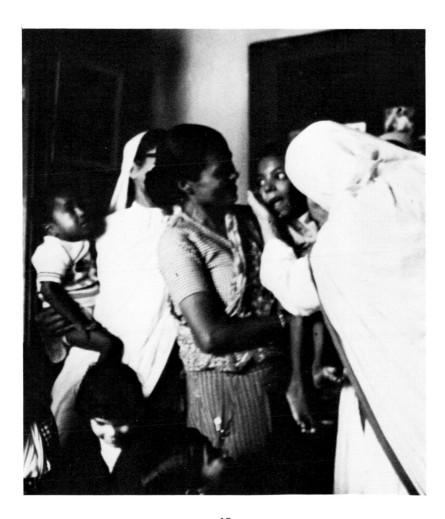

The best and surest way to learn the love of Jesus
is through the family.

We are created in the image of God
    in the image of Jesus as a human being.
Every child has been created for a greater thing
    —to love and be loved.
From the very beginning
from the time there is life
from the time there is conception
there is the life of God
    —the life of the living God.
That is why it is so wrong to destroy life
    —to destroy the image of God.

Whatever you do in your family
                for your children
                for your husband
                for your wife
        you do for Jesus.

Many of the troubles of modern society are caused by broken families. Many mothers and fathers are so busy that they are never home.

Children come home from school and there is no one
> to receive them
> to pay attention to them
> to encourage them if they are sad
> to share their joy if they are happy.

Children long for somebody
> to accept them
> to love them
> to praise them
> to be proud of them.

If they do not have this, they will go to the streets where there are plenty of people ready to accept them. The child can be lost. Much hatred and destruction is caused when a child is lost to the family.

Like our Lady and St. Joseph we must go and search for the child. When Jesus was lost they went and searched. They did not sit and wait. They did not rest until they found him.

We must bring the child back, make the child feel wanted.

Without the child there is no hope.

Love begins at home.
If we do not love one another who we see 24 hours
        how can we love those we see only once?
We show love by thoughtfulness
                by kindness
                by sharing joy
                by sharing a smile . . .
Through the little things.

A little child has no difficulty in loving
                has no obstacles to love.
And that is why Jesus said,
        "Unless you become like little children . . . ."

Once a lady came to me in great sorrow and told me that her daughter had lost her husband and a child. All the daughter's hatreds had turned on the mother. She wouldn't even see the mother.

So I said, "Now you think a bit about the little things that your daughter liked when she was a child. Maybe flowers or a special food. Try to give her some of these things without looking for a return."

And she started doing some of these things, like putting the daughter's favorite flower on the table, or leaving a beautiful piece of cloth for her. And she did not look for a return from the daughter.

Several days later the daughter said, "Mommy, come. I love you. I want you."

It was very beautiful.

By being reminded of the joy of childhood, the daughter reconnected with her family life. She must have had a happy childhood to go back to the joy and happiness of her mother's love.

It is very important for children to hear their parents talk about God. The children must be able to ask about God.

Once I gave a prayer to a communist and he took it back to his family and the children started to pray.

When he saw me again he said, "Mother, you don't know how your prayer and picture have disturbed the whole family. The children want to know who God is. They want to know why Mother is speaking this way."

The children are hungry.

That is why we need to pray together.

If the parent sets the example, the children will not forget how to pray

how they love each other
how they share sorrow
how they share joy.

Children watch . . . they watch
and they grow with that.

They will learn that it makes a difference how they live their lives by watching what the parents do.

If we can bring prayer into the family, the family will stay together. They will love one another. Just get together for five minutes.

Start with the Our Father, that's all!

Or we can say

"My Lord I love you
my God I am sorry
my God I believe in you
my God I trust you.
Help us to love one another
as you love us."

That is where your strength will come from
when you teach each other in prayer.

God has sent the family—together as husband and wife and children—to be his love.

I once picked up a child of six or seven in the street and took her to Shishu Bhavin (a children's home) and gave her a bath, some clothes and some nice food. That evening the child ran away.

We took the child in a second and a third time, and she ran away.

After the third time I sent a sister to follow her. The sister found the child sitting with her mother and sister under a tree. There was a little dish there and the mother was cooking food she had picked up from the streets.

They were cooking there
they were eating there
they were sleeping there.
It was their home.

And then we understood why the child ran away. The mother just loved that child. And the child loved the mother. They were so beautiful to each other.

The child said *"bari jabo"*—it was her home.

Her mother was her home.

Many factors in the industrial world suffocate the joy
of loving. People have too much and they want more.
They are discontent.

A family in Australia with six or seven children talked
together and decided not to buy a new television. They
wanted to enjoy each other more completely. They had
enough of what they needed for each other in each other.

Instead of buying the television, they gave the money
to me to do something for the poor Aborigines there.

They overcame something they thought divided them,
an obstacle to the joy of loving.

And they recognized the sharing
                          the talking
                          the laughing
                          the loving
                          the teasing.
The whole family is simply delighted.

We have hundreds of American and European young people coming here to join the Hindus. They are looking for something.

I always ask them if "Jesus is not enough for you?"

We have to try to give Jesus to our youth. They must be able to look up and see Jesus. And they must be able to see him in the home.

Six

Suffering —
the Kiss
of Jesus

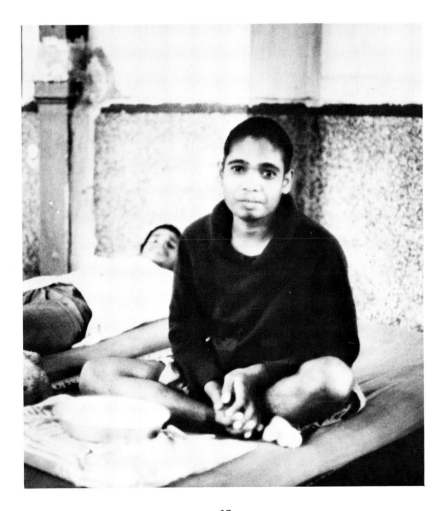

Suffering—
pain, humiliation, sickness and failure—
is but a kiss of Jesus.

Once I met a lady who had a terrible cancer.
She was suffering so much.
I told her,
    "Now you come so close to Jesus on the cross
    that he is kissing you."
Then she joined hands and said,
    "Mother Teresa,
    please tell Jesus to stop kissing me."
It was so beautiful.
She understood.

Suffering is a gift of God
a gift that makes us most Christlike.
People must not accept suffering as a punishment.

At Christmas I was talking to our lepers
and telling them that the leprosy is a gift from God.
That God can trust them so much
that he gives them this terrible suffering.
And they are so lonely,
like Jesus felt when he came.
He was also very lonely because
as a human being
he was away from the Father.

And one man
who was completely disfigured
started pulling at my sari.
    "Repeat that," he said.
    "Repeat that this is God's love.
    Those who are suffering understand you when you
        talk like this, Mother Teresa."

Christ is really living his passion in these homes.
In our people you can see Calvary.

We have a great people among us,
>only we do not know it.
They are the poorest of the poor—
>the unwanted
>the uncared for
>the rejected
>the alcoholics
>the crippled
>the blind
>the sick
>the dying—
people who have nothing and have nobody.

Their very life is a prayer.
They continually intercede for us
>without knowing it.
That's why I say that the Home for the Dying
>(in Calcutta)
is a treasure house for the whole archdiocese.
The people there intercede for us
>without knowing it.

Anyone who imitates Jesus to the full
must also share in his passion.

We must have the courage
to pray to have the courage to accept.
Because we do not pray enough, we see only the
        human part.
We don't see the divine.
And we resent it.

I think that much of the misunderstanding of suffering
        today
        comes from that
        from resentment and bitterness.
Bitterness is an infectious disease
        a cancer
        an anger hidden inside.

Suffering is meant to purify
        to sanctify
        to make us Christlike.

I wonder what the world would be like
if there were not these great people who continually
    suffer
  suffer with such dignity and love.

The dying man who said to one of our sisters,
  "I am going home to God."
He did not curse anybody.
He did not say anything about his difficulties
  only, "I am going home to God."
Then he closed his eyes
and went home.
Just as simple and beautiful as that.
He went home to Jesus.
He went home to see the face of God.
His heart was so pure and so beautiful.

We don't realize the greatness of the poor
and how much they give us.
It is a wonder.

We ask those who are about to die in the Home for the Dying if they want a blessing by which their sins will be forgiven and they will see God. If they say yes, we give them the blessing. We help them all die in peace with God. And everybody knows that we give them a ticket for St. Peter. I don't think anyone has died here without making peace with God.

Seven

Love Seeks to Serve

We are supposed to preach without preaching
not by words, but by our example, by our actions.
All works of love are works of peace.

This is the true reason for our existence
    to be the sunshine of God's love
    to be the hope of eternal happiness.
That's all.

We all want to love God, but how?

The Little Flower is a most wonderful example. She did small things with great love. Ordinary things with extraordinary love. That is why she became a great saint.

I think we can bring this beautiful thing into our lives.

Love cannot remain by itself—it has no meaning.
Love has to be put into action
and that action is service.

How do we put the love for God in action?
By being faithful to our family
    to the duties that God has entrusted to us.
Whatever form we are
    able or disabled
    rich or poor
it is not how much we do
but how much love we put in the doing
    —a lifelong sharing of love with others.

Jesus made himself the Bread of Life
>to make sure we understand what he is saying
>to satisfy our hunger for him
>to satisfy our love for him.

Even that is not enough for him
so he makes himself the hungry one
so we can satisfy his hunger for our love.
And by doing to the poor what we are doing
we are satisfying his hunger for our love.

How much smaller could he have made himself than a little piece of bread—the Bread of Life?

How much more weak and helpless?

And how much more ugly could he make himself than a badly diseased leper?

And yet it is he.

We must know it.

As I know that two and two make four, I must know that it is Jesus in that person.

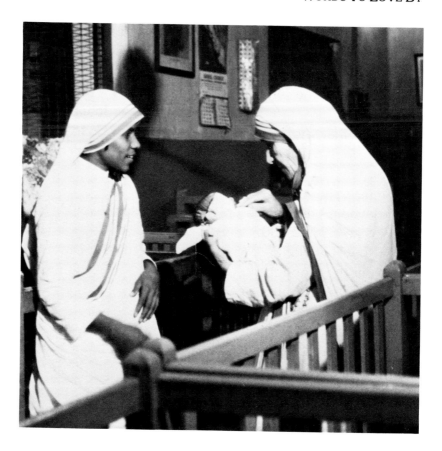

I never look at the masses as my responsibility.

I look at the individual. I can love only one person at a time. I can feed only one person at a time.

Just one, one, one.

You get closer to Christ by coming closer to each
        other. As Jesus said, "Whatever you do to the
        least of my brethren, you do to me."

So you begin . . . . I begin.

I picked up one person—

maybe if I didn't pick up that one person I wouldn't have picked up 42,000.

The whole work is only a drop in the ocean. But if I didn't put the drop in, the ocean would be one drop less.

Same thing for you
same thing in your family
same thing in the church where you go
just begin . . . one, one, one.

At the end of life we will not be judged by
how many diplomas we have received
how much money we have made
how many great things we have done.

We will be judged by
"I was hungry and you gave me to eat
I was naked and you clothed me
I was homeless and you took me in."

Hungry not only for bread
—but hungry for love
Naked not only for clothing
—but naked of human dignity and respect
Homeless not only for want of a room of bricks
—but homeless because of rejection.
This is Christ in distressing disguise.